SUSAN HOLBROOK

ink   *earl*

ERASURE POEMS

Coach House Books, Toronto

Canada Council **Conseil des Arts**
for the Arts **du Canada**

 ONTARIO ARTS COUNCIL
CONSEIL DES ARTS DE L'ONTARIO
an Ontario government agency
un organisme du gouvernement de l'Ontario

Canada

Published with the generous assistance of the Canada Council for the Arts and the Ontario Arts Council. Coach House Books also acknowledges the support of the Government of Canada through the Canada Book Fund and the Government of Ontario through the Ontario Book Publishing Tax Credit.

LIBRARY AND ARCHIVES CANADA CATALOGUING IN PUBLICATION
Title: Ink earl : erasure poems / Susan Holbrook.
Names: Holbrook, Susan, author.
Identifiers: Canadiana (print) 20210255536 | Canadiana (ebook) 20210255544 | ISBN 9781552454275 (softcover) | ISBN 9781770566781 (EPUB) | ISBN 9781770566798 (PDF)
Classification: LCC PS8565.O412 I55 2021 | DDC C811/.54—dc23

ink earl is available as an ebook: ISBN 978 1 77056 678 1 (EPUB); ISBN 978 1 77076 679 8 (PDF)

for you

for

stan

for everyone

Smudge resistant and easy to maneuver, Paper Mate® Pink Pearl® Erasers are the perfect partner for your writing.

- 100% latex-free and smudge-resistant eraser to keep your pages fresh
- Clean finish is perfect for exams, **essays** and everyday writing—a trusted choice for standardized tests
- Sharp corners and flat face help you erase both details and large areas
- Classic design is ideal for everyone from students to serious artists

love

Smudge resistant and easy to maneuver, Paper Mate® Pink Pearl® Erasers are the perfect partner for your writing.

- 100% latex-free and smudge-resistant eraser to keep your pages fresh
- Clean finish is perfect for exams, essays and everyday writing—a trusted choice for standardized tests
- Sharp corners and flat face help you erase both details and large areas
- Classic design is ideal for everyone from students to serious artists

Smudge resistant and easy to maneuver, Paper Mate® Pink Pearl® Erasers are the perfect partner for **you**r writing.

- 100% latex-free and smudge-resistant eraser to keep your pages fresh
- Clean finish is perfect for exams, essays a**n**d **ev**e**r**y**d**ay writing—a trusted choice for standardized tests
- Sharp corners and flat face help you erase both details and large areas
- Classic design **is** ideal for everyone from students to serious art**is**ts

Smudge resistant and easy to maneuver, Paper Mate® Pink Pearl® Erasers are **the perfect partner** for your writing.

- 100% latex-free and smudge-resistant eraser to keep your pages fresh
- Clean finish is perfect for exams, essays and everyday writing—a trusted choice for **standard**ized tests
- Sharp corners and flat **face** help you erase both details and **large** areas
- Classic design is ideal for everyone from students to **serious** artists

Smudge resistant and easy to **mane**uver, Paper Mate® Pink Pearl® Erasers are the perfect partner for your writing.

- 100% latex-free and smudge-resistant eraser **to** keep your pages fresh
- Clean finish is perfect for exams, essays and everyday writing—a trusted choice for standardized tests
- Sharp corners and flat face help you erase both de**tail**s and large **are**as
- **Classic** design is ide**al** for everyone from students to serious **art**ists

Smudge resistant and easy to maneuver, Paper Mate® Pink Pearl® Erasers are the perfect partner for your writing.

- 100% latex-free and smudge-resistant eraser to keep your pages fresh
- Clean finish is perfect for exams, essays and everyday writing—a trusted choice for standardized tests
- Sharp corners and flat face help **you** erase both details and large **are**as
- Classic design is ide**a**l for everyone from **stud**ents to serious artists

Smudge resistant and easy to maneuver, Paper Mate® Pink Pearl® Erasers are the perfect partner for your writing.

- 100% latex-free and smudge-resistant eraser to keep your pages fresh
- Clean finish is perfect for exams, essays and everyday writing—a trusted choice for standardized tests
- Sharp corners and flat face help you erase both details and large areas
- Classic design is ideal for everyone from students to serious artists

Smudge resistant and easy to maneuver, Paper Mate® Pink Pearl® Erasers are the perfect partner for **your** writing.

- 100% latex-free **and** smudge-resistant eraser to keep your pages fresh
- Clean finish is perfect for exams, essays and everyday writing—a trusted choice for standardized tests
- Sharp corners and flat face help you erase both details **and** large areas
- Classic design is ideal for everyone from students to serious artists

Smudge resistant **and** easy to maneuver, Paper Mate® Pink Pearl® Erasers are the perfect partner for **your** writing.

- 100% latex-free and smudge-resistant eraser to keep your pages fresh
- Clean finish is perfect for exams, essays and everyday writing—a trusted choice for standardized tests
- Sharp corners and flat face help you erase both details and large areas
- Classic design is ideal for everyone from students to serious artists

Smudge resistant and easy to maneuver, Paper Mate® Pink Pearl® Erasers are the perfect partner for **you**r w**r**iting.

- 100% latex-free and smudge-resistant eraser to keep your pages fresh
- Clean finish i**s** perfect for **ex**ams, essa**y**s and everyday writing—a trusted choice for standardized tests
- Sharp corners and flat face help you erase both details and large areas
- Classic design is ide**a**l for everyone **f**rom students to serious artists

P   l E ase

m   is t a   k e
       m e   for

       you r
l o   ver

the world

Smudge resistant and easy to maneuver, Paper Mate® Pink Pearl® Erasers are the perfect partner for your writing.

- 100% latex-free and smudge-resistant eraser to keep your pages fresh
- Clean finish is perfect for exams, essays and everyday writing—a trusted choice for standardized tests
- Sharp corners and flat face **help** you erase both details and large areas
- Classic design is ideal for everyone from students to serio**us** artists

Smudge resistant and easy to maneuver, Paper Mate® Pink Pearl® Erasers are the perfect partner for your writing.

- 100% latex-free and smudge-resistant eraser to keep your pages fresh
- Clean finish is perfect for exams, essays and everyday writing—a trusted choice for standardized tests
- Sharp corners and flat face help you erase both details and large areas
- Classic design is ideal for everyone from students to serious artists

Smudge resistant and easy to maneuver, Paper Mate® Pink Pearl® Erasers are **the** perfect partner for your writing.

- 100% latex-free and smudge-resistant eraser to keep your pages fresh
- Clean finish is perfect for exams, essays and everyday writing—a trusted choice for standardized tests
- Sharp corners and flat face help you erase both details and large areas
- Classic design is ideal for **everyone** from students to serious artists

Smudge **resist**ant and easy to maneuver, Paper Mate® Pink Pearl® Erasers are the perfect partner for your writing.

- 100% latex-free and smudge-resistant eraser to keep your pages fresh
- Clean finish is perfect for exams, essays and everyday writing—a trusted choice for standardized tests
- Sharp corners and flat face help you erase both details and large areas
- Classic design is ideal for everyone from students to serious artists

Smudge resistant and easy to maneuver, Paper Mate® Pink Pearl® Erasers are the perfect partner for your writing.

- 100% latex-free and smudge-resistant eraser to keep your pages fresh
- Clean finish is perfect for exams, essays and everyday writing—a trusted choice for standardized tests
- Sharp corners and flat face help you erase both details and large areas
- Classic design is ideal for everyone from students to serious artists

Smudge resistant and easy to **man**euver, Paper Mate® Pink Pearl® **Eraser**s are the perfect partner for your writing.

- 100% latex-free and smudge-resistant eraser to keep your pages fresh
- Clean finish is perfect for exams, essays and everyday writing—a trusted cho**ice** for st**and**ar**dize**d tests
- Sharp corners and flat face help you erase both details and large areas
- Classic design is ideal for everyone from students to serious artists

Smudge resistant and easy to maneuver, Paper Mate® Pink Pearl® Erasers are the perfect partner for your writing.

- 100% latex-free and smudge-resistant eraser to keep your pages **fresh**
- Clean finish is perfect for exams, essays and everyday writing—a trusted choice for standardized tests
- Sharp corners and flat face help you erase both details and large areas
- Classic design is ideal for everyone from students to serious artists

Smudge resistant and easy to maneuver, **P**aper Mate® Pink Pearl® Erasers are the perfect partner for your writing.

- 100% latex-free and smudge-resistant eraser to keep your pages fresh
- Clean finish is perfect for exams, essays and everyday writing—a trusted choice for standardized tests
- Sharp corners and flat face help you erase both details and large areas
- Classic design is ideal for everyone from students to serious artists

Smudge resistant and easy to maneuver, Paper Mate® Pink Pearl® Erasers are the perfect partner for your writing.

- 100% latex-free and smudge-resistant eraser to **keep** your pages fresh
- Clean finish is perfect for exams, essays and everyday writing—a tr**us**ted choice for standardized tests
- Sharp corners and flat face help you erase both details and large areas
- Classic design is ideal for everyone **from** students to serio**us** artists

Smudge resistant and easy to maneuver, Paper Mate® Pink Pearl® **Erase**rs are the perfect partner for **your writing.**

- 100% latex-free and smudge-resistant eraser to keep your pages fresh
- Clean finish is perfect for exams, essays and everyday writing—a trusted choice for standardized tests
- Sharp corners and flat face help you erase both details and large areas
- Classic design is ideal for everyone from students to serious artists

Smudge resistant and easy to maneuver, Paper Mate® Pink Pearl® Erasers are the perfect partner for your writing.

- 100% latex-free and smudge-resistant **erase**r to keep **your** pages fresh
- Clean finish is perfect for exams, essays and everyday writing—a trusted choice for standardized tests
- Sharp corners and flat face help you erase both details and large areas
- Classic design is ideal for everyone from students to serious artists

Smudge resistant and **easy** to maneuver, Paper Mate® Pink **Pearl**® Erasers are the perfect partner for your writing.

- 100% latex-free and smudge-resistant eraser **to ke**ep your pages fresh
- Clean finish is perfec**t fo**r exams, essays and everyday writing—a trusted choice for standardized tests
- Sharp corners and flat face **help you** erase both details and large areas
- Classic design is **idea**l for everyone from students to serious artists

Smudge resistant and easy to maneuver, Paper Mate® Pink Pearl® Erasers are the perfect partner for your writing.

- 100% latex-free and smudge-resistant eraser to keep your pages fresh
- Clean finish is perfect for exams, essays and everyday writing—a trusted choice for standardized tests
- Sharp corners and flat face help you erase both details and large areas
- Classic design is ideal for everyone from students to serious artists

Smudge resistant and easy to maneuver, Paper Mate® Pink Pearl® Erasers are the perfect partner for your writing.

- 100% latex-free and smudge-resistant eraser to keep your pages fresh
- Clean finish is perfect for exams, essays and everyday writing—a trusted choice for standardized tests
- Sharp corners and flat face help you erase both details and large areas
- Classic design is ideal for everyone from students to serious artists

Smudge resistant and easy to maneuver, Paper Mate® Pink Pearl® Erasers are the perfect partner for your writing.

- 100% latex-free and smudge-resistant eraser to keep your pages fresh
- Clean finish is perfect for exams, essays and everyday writing—a trusted choice for standardized tests
- Sharp corners and flat face help you erase both details and large areas
- Classic design is ideal for everyone from students to serious artists

Smudge resistant and easy to maneuver, Paper Mate® Pink Pearl® Erasers are the perfect partner for your writing.

- 100% latex-free and smudge-resistant eraser to keep your pages fresh
- Clean finish is perfect for exams, essays and everyday writing—a trusted choice for standardized tests
- Sharp corners and flat face help you erase both details and large areas
- Classic design is ideal for everyone from students to serious artists

Smudge resistant and easy to maneuver, Paper Mate® Pink Pearl® Erasers are the perfect partner for your writing.

- 100% latex-free and smudge-resistant eraser to keep your pages fresh
- Clean finish is perfect for exams, essays and everyday writing—a trusted choice for standardized tests
- Sharp corners and flat face help you erase both details and large areas
- Classic design is ideal for everyone from students to serious artists

Smudge resistant and easy to maneuver, Paper Mate® Pink Pearl® Erasers are the perfect partner for your writing.

- 100% latex-**free** and smudge-resistant eraser to keep your pages fresh
- Clean finish is perfect for exams, essays and everyday writing—a trusted choice for standardized tests
- Sharp corners and flat face help you erase both details and large areas
- Classic design is ideal for **everyone from** students to **serious** artists

trust

you

food

Smudge resistant and easy to maneuver, Paper Mate® Pink Pearl® Erasers are the perfect partner for your writing.

- 100% latex-free and smudge-resistant eraser to keep your pages fresh
- Clean finish is perfect for exams, essays and everyday writing—a trusted choice for standardized tests
- Sharp corners and flat face help you erase both details and large areas
- Classic design is ideal for everyone from students to serious artists

Smudge resistant and easy to maneuver, Paper Mate® Pink Pearl® Erasers are the perfect partner for your writing.

- 100% latex-free and smudge-resistant eraser to keep your pages fresh
- Clean finish is perfect for exams, essays and everyday writing—a trusted choice for standardized tests
- Sharp corners and flat face help you erase both details and large areas
- Classic design is ideal for everyone from students to serious artists

Smudge resistant and easy to maneuver, Paper Mate® Pink Pearl® Erasers are the perfect partner for your writing.

- 100% latex-free and smudge-resistant eraser to keep your pages fresh
- Clean finish is perfect for exams, essays and everyday writing—a trusted choice for standardized tests
- Sharp corners and flat **face** help you erase both details and large areas
- Classic design is ideal for everyone from students to serious artists

Smudge resistant and easy to maneuver, Paper Mate® Pink Pearl® Erasers are the perfect partner for your writing.

- 100% latex-free and smudge-resistant eraser to keep your pages fresh
- Clean **finish** is perfect for exams, essays and everyday writing—a trusted choice for standardized tests
- Sharp **corn**ers and flat face help you erase both details and large areas
- Classic design is ideal for everyone from students to serious artists

Smudge resistant and easy to maneuver, Paper Mate® Pink Pearl® Erasers are the perfect partner for your writing.

- 100% latex-free and smudge-resistant eraser to keep your pages fresh
- Clean finish is perfect for exams, essays and everyday writing—a trusted choice for standardized tests
- Sharp corners and flat face help you erase both details and large areas
- Classic design is ideal for everyone from students to serious artists

Smudge resistant and easy to maneuver, Paper Mate® Pink Pearl® Erasers are the perfect partner for your writing.

- 100% latex-free and smudge-resistant eraser to keep your pages fresh
- Clean **finish** is perfect for exams, essays and everyday writing—a trusted choice for standardized tests
- Sharp **corners** and flat face help you erase both details and large areas
- Classic design is ideal for everyone from students to serious artists

Smudge resistant and **easy** to mane**uver**, Paper Mate® Pink Pearl® Erasers are the perfect partner for your writing.

- 100% latex-free and smudge-resistant eraser to keep your pages fresh
- Clean finish is perfect f**or** exams, essays and everyday writing—a trusted choice for standardized tests
- Sh**a**rp corn**e**rs and flat fa**c**e help you erase **b**oth details and **l**arge areas
- Classic **d**esign is ideal for everyone fro**m** students to s**e**r**i**ous artist**s**

Smudge resistant and easy to maneuver, Paper Mate® Pink Pearl® Erasers are the perfect partner for your writing.

- 100% latex-free and smudge-resistant eraser to keep your pages fresh
- Clean **finish** is perfect for exams, essays and everyday writing—a trusted choice for standardized tests
- Sharp corners **and flat fa**ce help you erase both details and large areas
- Classic design is ideal for everyone from students to serious artists

Smudge resistant and easy to maneuver, Paper Mate® Pink Pearl® Erasers are the perfect partner for your writing.

- **100%** latex-free and smudge-resistant eraser to keep your pages **fresh**
- Clean finish is perfect for exams, essays and everyday writing—a trusted choice for standardized tests
- Sharp corners and flat face **hel**p you erase both details and large areas
- Classic design is ideal for everyone from students to serious artists

m

m

M

m

m

m

art

Smudge resistant and easy to maneuver, Paper Mate® Pink Pearl® Erasers are the perfect partner for your writing.

- 100% latex-free and smudge-resistant eraser to keep your pages fresh
- Clean finish is perfect for exams, essays and everyday writing—a trusted choice for standardized tests
- Sharp corners and flat face help you erase both details and large areas
- Classic design is ideal for everyone from students to serious artists

Smudge resistant and easy to maneuver, Paper Mate® Pink Pearl® Erasers are the perfect partner for your writing.

- 100% latex-free and smudge-resistant eraser to keep your pages fresh
- Clean finish is perfect for exams, essays and everyday writing—a trusted choice for standardized tests
- Sharp corners and flat face help you erase both details and large areas
- **Classic** design is ideal for everyone from students to serious artists

Smudge resistant and easy to maneuver, Paper Mate® Pink Pearl® Erasers are the perfect partner for your writing.

- 100% latex-free and s**mud**ge-res**i**sta**nt** eraser to keep **your** pages fresh
- Clean finish is perfect for exams, essays and everyday writing—a trusted choice for standardized tests
- Sharp corners and flat **face** help you erase both details **and** large areas
- Classic de**sign** is ideal for everyone from students to serious art**is**ts

Smudge resistant and easy to maneuver, Paper Mate® Pink Pearl® Erasers are the perfect partner for your writing.

- 100% latex-free and smudge-resistant eraser to keep your pages fresh
- **Clean** finish is perfect for exams, essays and everyday writing—a trusted choice for standardized tests
- Sharp corners and flat **face** help you erase both details **and** large areas
- Classic de**sign** is ideal for everyone from students to serious artists

Smudge resistant and easy to **maneuver**, Paper Mate® Pink **Pearl**® Erasers are the perfect partner for your writing.

- 100% latex-free and smudge-resistant eraser **to** keep your pages fresh
- Clean finish is perfect for exams, essays and everyday writing—a trusted choice for standardized tests
- Sharp **corner**s and flat face help you erase both details **and** large areas
- Classic de**sign** is ideal for everyone from students to serious artists

Smudge resistant and easy to maneuver, Paper **Ma**te® Pin**k** P**e**arl® Erasers are the perfect partner for your writing.

- 100% latex-**free** a**nd s**mudge-resistant eraser to keep your pages fresh
- Clean finish is perfect for exams, essays and everyday writing—a trusted choice for st**and**ardized tests
- Sharp corners and flat face help you erase both details and large areas
- Classic de**sign** is ideal for everyon**e** fro**m** students to serious artists

Smudge resistant and easy to maneuver, Paper Mate® Pink Pearl® **Erase**rs are the perfect partner for your writing.

- 100% latex-free **an**d smudge-resistant **eraser** to keep your pages fresh
- Clean finish is perfect for exams, essays and everyday writing—a trusted choice for stand**ard**ized tests
- Sharp corners and flat face help you erase both details **and** large areas
- Classic de**sign** is ideal for everyone from students to serious art**is**ts

Smudge resistant and easy to maneuver, Paper Mate® Pink Pearl® Erasers are the perfect partner for your writing.

- 100% latex-free and smudge-resistant eraser to keep your pages fresh
- Clean finish is perfect for exams, essays and everyday writing—a trusted choice for standardized tests
- Sharp corners and flat face help you erase both details and large areas
- Classic design is ideal for everyone from students to serious artists

Smudge resistant and easy to maneuver, Paper Mate® Pink Pearl® Erasers are the perfect partner for your writing.

- 100% latex-free and smudge-resistant eraser to keep your pages fresh
- Clean finish is perfect for exams, essays and everyday writing—a trusted choice for standardized tests
- Sharp corners and flat face help you erase both details and large areas
- Classic design s ideal for everyone from students to serious artists

family

Smudge resistant and easy to maneuver, Paper Mate® Pink **Pearl**® Erasers are the perfect partner for your writing.

- 100% latex-free **and** smudge-resistant eraser to keep your pages fresh
- Clean finish is perfect for exams, essays and everyday writing—a trusted choice for standardiz**ed** tests
- Sharp corners and flat face help you erase both details **and** large areas
- Classic **desi**gn is ideal for everyone from students to serious artists

Smudge resistant **and** easy to maneuver, Paper **Ma**te® Pink Pearl® Erasers are the perfect partner for your writing.

- 100% latex-free **and** smudge-resist**ant** eraser to keep your **page**s fresh
- Clean finish is perfect for exams, essays and everyday writing—a trusted choice for st**and**ardized **test**s
- Sharp corners **and** flat face help you erase both details and large areas
- Classic design is ide**al f**or everyone from students to serious artists

Smudge resistant **and** easy to maneuver, **Pa**per Mate® Pink Pearl® Erasers are the perfect partner for your writing.

- 100% latex-free **and** smudge-resistant eraser to keep **your pa**ges fresh
- Clean finish is perfect for exams, **essa**ys **and** everyday writ**ing—a** trusted **cho**ice for st**and**ar**di**zed tests
- Sharp corners **and** flat face he**l**p y**ou** erase both d**et**ails and large areas
- Classic design is ide**al** for everyone from students to serious artists

Smudge resistant and easy to maneuver, Paper Mate® Pink Pearl® Erasers are the perfect partner for your writing.

- 100% latex-free and smudge-resistant eraser to keep your pages fresh
- Clean finish is perfect for exams, essays and everyday writing—a trusted choice for standardized tests
- Sharp corners and flat face help you erase both details and large areas
- Classic design is ideal for everyone from students to serious artists

Smudge resistant and easy to maneuver, Paper Mate® Pink Pearl® Erasers are the perfect partner for your writing.

- 100% latex-free **and** smudge-resistant eraser to keep your pages fresh
- Clean finish is perfect fo**r ex**ams, essays and everyday writing—a trusted choice for st**and**ardized tests
- Sharp corners and flat face help you erase both details and large areas
- C**lassi**c design is ideal for everyone from students to serious artists

Smudge resistant **and** easy to maneuver, Paper Mate® Pink Pearl® Erasers are the perfect partner for your writing.

- 100% latex-free and smudge-resistant eraser **to** keep your pages fresh
- Clean finish is perfect for exams, essays and everyday writing—a trusted choice for standardized tests
- Sharp corners and flat face help you erase both details and large areas
- Classic design is ideal for everyone from students **to** serious artists

Smudge resistant **and** easy to maneuver, Paper Mate® Pink Pearl® Erasers are the perfect partner for your writing.

- **100**% latex-free **and** smudge-resistant eraser to keep your pages fresh
- Clean finish is perfect for exams, essays and everyday writing—a trusted choice for standardized tests
- Sharp corners and flat face help you erase both details and large areas
- Classic design is ideal for everyone from students to serious artists

Smudge resistant and easy to maneuver, Paper Mate® Pink Pearl® Erasers are the perfect partner for your writing.

- 100% latex-free and smudge-resistant eraser to keep your pages fresh
- Clean finish is perfect for exams, essays and everyday writing—a trusted **choice** for standardized tests
- Sharp corners and flat face help you erase both details and large areas
- Classic design is ideal for everyone from students to serious artists

Smudge resistant and easy to maneuver, Paper Mate® Pink Pearl® Erasers are the perfect partner for your writing.

- 100% latex-free and smudge-resistant eraser to keep your pages fresh
- Clean finish is perfect for exams, essays and everyday writing—a trusted choice for standardized tests
- Sharp corners and flat face help you erase both details and large areas
- Classic design is ideal for everyone from students to serious artists

I   sis
                    for   every

        lass

music

Smudge resistant and easy to maneuver, Paper Mate® Pink Pearl® Erasers are the perfect partner for your writing.

- 100% latex-free **and** smudge-resistant eraser to keep your pages fresh
- Clean finish is perfect for exams, essays and everyday **writing**—a trusted choice for **stand**ardized tests
- Sharp corners and flat face help you erase both details and large areas
- Classic design is **ide**al for everyone from students to serious artists

Smudge resistant and easy to maneuver, Paper Mate® Pink Pearl® Erasers are the perfect partner for your writing.

- 100% latex-free and smudge-resistant eraser to keep your pages fresh
- Clean finish is perfect for exams, essays and everyday writing—a trusted choice for standardized tests
- Sharp corners and flat face help you erase both details and large areas
- Classic design is ideal for everyone from students to serious artists

Smudge resistant **and** easy to maneuver, Paper Mate® Pink Pearl® Erasers are the perfect partner for your writing.

- 100% latex-free and smudge-resistant eraser to keep your pages fresh
- Clean finish is perfect for exams, essays and everyday writing—a trusted choice **for** standardized tests
- Sharp corners **and** flat face help you erase both details and large areas
- Classic design is ideal for **everyone** from students to serious artists

Smudge resistant and easy to maneuver, Paper Mate® Pink Pearl® Erasers are the perfect partner for your writing.

- 100% latex-free and smudge-resistant eraser to keep your pages fresh
- Clean finish is perfect for exams, essays and everyday writing—a trusted choice for standardized tests
- Sharp corners and flat face help you erase both details and large areas
- Classic design is ideal for everyone from students to serious artists

Smudge resistant and easy to maneuver, Paper Mate® Pink Pearl® Erasers are the perfect partner for your writing.

- 100% latex-free and smudge-resistant eraser to keep your pages fresh
- Clean finish is perfect for exams, essays and everyday writing—a trusted choice for standardized tests
- Sharp corners and d flat face help you erase both details and large areas
- Classic design is ideal for everyone from students to serious artists

Smudge resistant and easy to maneuver, Paper Mate® Pink Pearl® Erasers are the perfect partner for your writing.

- 100% latex-free and smudge-resistant eraser to keep your pages fresh
- Clean finish is perfect for exams, essays and everyday writing--a trusted choice for standardized tests
- **Sharp** corners and flat face help you erase both details and large areas
- Classic design is ideal for everyone from students to serious artists

Smudge resistant and easy to maneuver, Paper Mate® Pink Pearl® Erasers are the perfect partner for your writing.

- 100% latex-free and smudge-resistant eraser to keep your pages fresh
- Clean finish is perfect for exams, essays and everyday writing—a trusted choice for standardized tests
- Sharp corners and flat face help you erase both details and large areas
- Classic design is ideal for everyone from students to serious artists

Smudge resistant and easy to maneuver, Paper Mate® **Pink** Pearl® Erasers are the perfect partner for your writing.

- 100% latex-free and smudge-resistant e**rase**r to keep **your** pages fresh
- Clean finish is perfect for exams, essays and everyday writing—a trusted choice for standardized tests
- Sharp corners and flat face help you erase both details and lar**g**e areas
- C**lass**ic design is ideal for everyone from students to serious artists

Smudge resistant and easy to maneuver, Paper Mate® Pink Pearl® Erasers are the perfect partner for your writing.

- 100% latex-free and smudge-resistant eraser to keep your pages fresh
- Clean finish is perfect for exams, essays and everyday writing—a trusted choice for standardized tests
- Sharp corners and flat face help you erase both details and large areas
- Classic design is ideal for everyone from students to serious artists

n   u   n   s   fre
                                          t

              n   o   t

health

Smudge resistant and easy to maneuver, Paper Mate® Pink Pearl® Erasers are the perfect partner for your writing.

- 100% latex-free and smudge-resistant eraser to keep your pages fresh
- Clean finish is perfect for exams, essays and everyday writing—a trusted choice for standardized tests
- Sharp corners and flat face help you erase both details and large areas
- Classic design is ideal for everyone from students to serious artists

Smudge resistant and easy to maneuver, Paper Mate® Pink Pearl® Erasers are the perfect partner for your writing.

- 100% latex-free and smudge-resistant eraser to keep your pages fresh
- Clean finish is perfect for exams, essays and everyday writing—a trusted choice for standardized tests
- Sharp corners and flat face help you erase both details and large areas
- Classic design is ideal for everyone from students to serious artists

Smudge resistant and easy to maneuver, Paper Mate® Pink Pearl® Erasers are the perfect partner for your writing.

- 100% latex-free and smudge-resistant eraser to keep your pages fresh
- Clean finish is perfect for exams, essays and everyday writing—a trusted choice for standardized tests
- Sharp corners and flat face help you erase both details and large areas
- Classic design is ideal for everyone from students to serious artists

Smudge resistant and easy to maneuver, Paper **Mate**® Pink Pearl® Erasers are the perfect partner for your writing.

- 100% **latex-free** and smudge-resistant eraser to keep your pages fresh
- Clean finish is perfect **for** exams, essays and everyday writing—a trusted choice for standardized tests
- Sharp corners and flat face help you erase both details and large areas
- Classic design is ideal for everyone from students to serious artists

Smudge resistant and easy to maneuver, **Pap**er Mate® Pink Pearl® Erasers are the perfect partner for your writing.

- 100% latex-free and smudge-resistant eraser to keep your pages fresh
- Clean finish is perfect for exams, essays and everyday writing—a trusted choice for standardized **tests**
- Sharp corners and flat face help you erase both details and large areas
- Classic design is ideal **for everyone** from students to serious artists

Smudge resistant and easy to maneuver, Paper Mate® Pink Pearl® Erasers are the perfect partner for **your** writing.

- 100% latex-free and smudge-resistant eraser to keep you**r** pa**ge**s fresh
- Clean finish is perfect fo**r** e**x**a**ms**, essays and everyday writing—a trusted choice for standardized tests
- Sharp corners and flat face help **you** erase both details and large areas
- Classic design is ideal for everyone from students to seri**ou**s ar**t**ists

Smudge resistant and easy to maneuver, Paper Mate® Pink Pearl® Erasers are the perfect partner for your writing.

- 100% latex-free and smudge-resistant eraser to keep your pages fresh
- Clean finish is perfect for exams, essays and everyday writing—a trusted choice for standardized tests
- Sharp corners and flat face help you erase both details and large areas
- Classic design is ideal for everyone from students to serious artists

Smudge resistant and easy to maneuver, Paper Mate® Pink Pearl® Erasers are the perfect partner for your writing.

- 100% latex-free and smudge-resistant eraser to keep your pages fresh
- Clean finish is perfect for exams, essays and everyday writing—a trusted choice for standardized tests
- Sharp corners and flat face help you erase both details and large areas
- Classic design is ideal for everyone from students to serious artists

Smudge resistant and easy to maneuver, Paper Mate® Pink Pearl® Erasers are the perfect partner for your writing.

- 100% latex-free and smudge-resistant eraser to keep your pages fresh
- Clean finish is perfect for exams, essays and everyday writing—a trusted choice for standardized tests
- Sharp corners and flat face help you erase both details and large areas
- Classic design is ideal for everyone from students to serious artist

d   res s
        your

            face
                ve   n   t   s

nature

Smudge resistant and easy to maneuver, Paper Mate® Pink Pearl® Erasers are the perfect partner for your writing.

- 100% latex-free and smudge-resistant eraser to keep your pages fresh
- Clean finish is perfect for exams, essays and everyday writing—a trusted choice for standardized tests
- Sharp corners and flat face help you erase both details and large areas
- Classic design is ideal for everyone from students to serious artists

Smudge resistant **and** easy to maneuver, Paper Mate® Pink Pearl® Erasers are the perfect partner for your writing.

- 100% latex-free and smudge-resistant eraser to keep your pages fresh
- Clean finish is perfect for exams, essays and everyday writing—a trusted choice for standardized tests
- Sharp corners and flat face help you erase both details and large areas
- Classic design is ideal for everyone from students to serious artists

Smudge resistant and easy to maneuver, Paper Mate® Pink Pearl® Erasers are the perfect partner for your writing.

- 100% latex-free and smudge-resistant eraser to keep **your** pages fresh
- Clean finish is perfect for exams, essays and everyday writing—a trusted choice for standardized tests
- Sharp corners and flat face help you erase both details and large areas
- Classic design is ideal for everyone from students to serious artists

Smudge resistant and easy to maneuver, Paper Mate® Pink Pearl® Erasers are the perfect partner for your writing.

- 100% latex-free and smudge-resistant eraser to keep your pages fresh
- Clean finish is perfect for exams, essays and everyday writing—a trusted choice for standardized tests
- Sharp corners and flat face help you erase both details and large areas
- Classic design is ideal for everyone from students to serious artists

Smudge resistant **and** easy to maneuver, Paper Mate® **Pink Pear**l® Erasers are the perfect partner for your writing.

- 100% latex-free and smudge-resistant eraser to keep your pages fresh
- Clean finish is perfect for exams, es**says** and everyday writing—a trusted choice for standardized tests
- Sharp corners and flat face help you erase both details and large areas
- Classic design is ideal for everyone from students to serious artists

Smudge resistant and easy to maneuver, Paper Mate® Pink Pearl® Erasers are the perfect partner for your writing.

- 100% latex-free and smudge-resistant eraser to keep your pages fresh
- Clean finish is perfect for exams, essays and everyday writing—a trusted choice for standardized tests
- Sharp corners and flat face help you erase both details and large areas
- Classic design is ideal for everyone from students to serious artists

Smudge resistant and easy **to** maneuver, Paper Mate® Pink Pearl® Erasers are the perfect partner for your **writ**ing.

- 100% latex-free and smudge-resistant eraser **to** keep your pages fresh
- Clean finish is perfect for exams, essays and everyday **w**riting—a trusted ch**o**ice f**o**r standardized tests
- Sharp corners and flat face help **you** erase both details and large areas
- Classic design is ideal for everyone from students to serious artists

Smudge resistant and easy to maneuver, Paper Mate® Pink Pearl® Erasers are the perfect partner for your **writing**.

- 100% latex-free and smudge-resistant eraser to keep your pages fresh
- Clean finish is perfect for exams, essays and everyday **writing**—a trusted choice for standardized tests
- Sharp corners and flat face help you erase both details and large areas
- Classic design is ideal for everyone from students to serious artists

Smudge resistant and easy to maneuver, Paper Mate® Pink Pearl® Erasers are the perfect partner for your writing.

- 100% latex-free and smudge-resistant eraser to keep your pages fresh
- Clean finish is perfect for exams, essays and everyday writing—a trusted choice for standardized tests
- Sharp corners and flat face help you erase both details and large areas
- Classic design is ideal for everyone from students to serious artists

S   i   s   e

          u

                    n   r
                         s   n

                              u   e
          s   t

thinkers

Smudge resistant and easy to maneuver, Paper Mate® Pink Pearl® Erasers are the perfect partner for your writing.

- 100% latex-free and smudge-resistant eraser to keep your pages fresh
- **Clean** finish is perfect for exams, essay**s and** everyday writing—a trusted choice for standardized tests
- Sharp corners and flat face help you erase both details and large areas
- Classic design is ideal for everyone from students to serious artists

Smudge resistant and easy to maneuver, Paper Mate® Pink Pearl® Erasers are the perfect partner for your writing.

- 100% latex-free and smudge-resistant eraser to keep your pages fresh
- Clean finish is perfect for exams, essays and everyday **writ**ing—a trusted choice for standardized tests
- Sharp corners and flat face help you erase both details and **large** areas
- Classic design **is** ideal for every**o**ne from stude**n**ts to s**e**rious artists

Smudge resistant and easy to maneuver, **Paper** Mate® Pink Pearl® Erasers are the perfect partner for your writing.

- 100% latex-free and smudge-resistant eraser to keep your pages fresh
- Clean finish is perfect for exams, essays and everyday writing—a trusted choice for standardized tests
- Sharp corners and **flat** face help you erase both details and large areas
- Classic design is ideal for everyone from students to serious artists

Smudge resistant and easy to maneuver, Paper Mate® Pink Pearl® Erasers are the perfect partner for **you**r writing.

- 100% latex-free and smudge-resistant eraser to keep your pages fresh
- Clean finish is perfect for exams, essays and everyday writing—**a tr**ust**e**d choice for standardized tests
- Sharp corners and flat face help you erase **bot**h details and large areas
- **Classic** design is ideal for everyone from students to serious artists

Smudge resistant and easy to maneuver, **Paper Mate**® Pink Pearl® Erasers are the perfect partner for your writing.

- 100% latex-free and smudge-resistant eraser to keep your pages fresh
- Clean finish is perfect for exams, essays and everyday writing—a trusted choice for standardized tests
- Sharp corners and flat face help you erase both details and large areas
- Classic design is ideal for everyone from students to serious artists

Smudge resistant and easy to maneuver, Paper Mate® Pink Pearl® Erasers are **the** perfect partner for your writing.

- 100% latex-free and smudge-resistant eraser to keep your pages fresh
- Clean **fin**ish is perfect for exams, essays and everyday writing—a trusted choice for standardized t**est**s
- Sharp corners and flat face help you erase both details and la**rge** areas
- Classic design **is** ideal for everyone **from** students to serious artists

Smudge resistant and easy to maneuver, Paper Mate® Pink Pearl® Erasers are the perfect partner for your writing.

- 100% latex-free and smudge-resistant eraser to keep your pages fresh
- Clean finish is perfect for exams, essays and everyday writing—a trusted choice for standardized tests
- Sharp corners and flat face help you erase both details and large areas
- Classic design is ideal for everyone from students to serious artists

Smudge resistant and easy to **man**euver, Paper Mate® Pink Pearl® Erasers are the perfect partner for your writing.

- 100% latex-free and smudge-res**is**tant eraser to keep your pages fresh
- Clean finish is perfect for exams, essays **an**d everyday writing—a trusted choice for standardized tests
- Sharp corners and flat face help you erase both deta**ils and** large areas
- Classic design is ideal for everyo**n**e fr**o**m **st**udents to serious artists

Smudge resistant and easy to maneuver, Paper Mate® Pink Pearl® Erasers are the **perfect** partner for your writing.

- 100% latex-free and smudge-resistant eraser to keep your pages fresh
- Clean fin**ish** is perfect for exams, essays and everyday writing—a trusted choice for standardized tests
- Sharp corners and flat face help you erase both details and large areas
- Classic design **is ideal** for everyone from students to serious artists

i

is

everyone

Smudge resistant and easy to maneuver, Paper Mate® Pink Pearl® Erasers are the perfect partner for your writing.

- 100% latex-free and smudge-resistant eraser to keep your pages fresh
- Clean **fin**ish is perfect for exams, essays and everyday writing—a trusted choice for standardized tests
- Sharp corners and flat face help you erase both details and large areas
- Classic design is ideal for everyone from students to serious artists

Smudge resistant and easy to maneuver, Paper Mate® Pink Pearl® Erasers are the perfect partner for your writing.

- 100% latex-free and smudge-resistant eraser to keep your pages fresh
- Clean finish is perfect for exams, essays and everyday writing—a trusted choice for standardized tests
- Sharp corners and flat face help you erase both details and large areas
- Classic design is ideal for everyone from students to serious artists

Smudge resistant and easy to maneuver, Paper Mate® Pink Pearl® Erasers are the perfect partner for your writing.

- 100% latex-free and smudge-resistant eraser to keep your pages fresh
- Clean finish is perfect for exams, essays and everyday writing—a trusted choice for standardized tests
- Sharp corners and flat face help you erase both details and large areas
- Classic design is ideal for everyone from students to serious artists

acknowledgements

Thank you to all the amazing people at corners and flat face help help you erase for making
this book with me. For all your fabulous ideas and care and artistry, thank you
details and large, corners and flat face help you erase both details, smudge-resistant
exams, essays,
easy to maneuver, Paper Mate® Pink Pearl® Erasers, details and large areas
• Classic design is ideal.

Thanks to my brother writing—a trusted choice for for the digital animation of love.

Thank you to brilliant readers who helped me erase: finish is perfect, smudge-resistant eraser,
and help you erase both details and large.

Endless gratitude to resistant and easy resistant and easy resitant and easy! for editorial genius and for the 100 Pink Pearl erasers you sent across the ocean, every P rubbed off.

Susan Holbrook's poetry books are the Governor General's Award–nominated and Trillium Book Award–nominated *Throaty Wipes*; *Joy Is So Exhausting*, which was shortlisted for the Trillium Award for Poetry; and *misled*, which was shortlisted for the Pat Lowther Memorial Award and the Stephan G. Stephansson Award. She lives in Leamington, Ontario.

Typeset in Aragon and Parisienne.

Printed at the Coach House on bpNichol Lane in Toronto, Ontario, on Cougar Opaque Natural paper. This book was printed with vegetable-based ink on a 1973 Heidelberg KORD offset litho press. Its pages were folded on a Baumfolder, gathered by hand, bound on a Sulby Auto-Minabinda, and trimmed on a Polar single-knife cutter.

Coach House is on the traditional territory of many nations, including the Mississaugas of the Credit, the Anishnabeg, the Chippewa, the Haudenosaunee, and the Wendat peoples, and is now home to many diverse First Nations, Inuit, and Métis peoples. We acknowledge that Toronto is covered by Treaty 13 with the Mississaugas of the Credit. We are grateful to live and work on this land.

Edited by Nasser Hussain. Cover and interior design by Crystal Sikma.

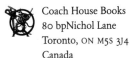 Coach House Books
80 bpNichol Lane
Toronto, ON M5S 3J4
Canada

416 979 2217 | 800 367 6360
mail@chbooks.com | www.chbooks.com